Australian Animals
Tasmanian Devils

by Lyn A. Sirota

Consulting Editor: Gail Saunders-Smith, PhD

Content Consultant: Nicole Dyble
Animal Keeper/Tour Guide
Devils@Cradle Tasmanian Devil Sanctuary, Cradle Mountain, Tasmania

CAPSTONE PRESS
a capstone imprint

Pebble Plus is published by Capstone Press,
151 Good Counsel Drive, P.O. Box 669, Mankato, Minnesota 56002.
www.capstonepress.com

092009
005618CGS10

 Books published by Capstone Press are manufactured with paper containing at least 10 percent
post-consumer waste.

Library of Congress Cataloging-in-Publication Data
Sirota, Lyn A., 1963–
    Tasmanian devils / by Lyn A. Sirota.
    p. cm. — (Pebble plus. Australian animals)
    Includes bibliographical references and index.
    Summary: "Simple text and photographs present Tasmanian devils, their physical features, where they live, and
what they do" — Provided by publisher.
    ISBN 978-1-4296-4506-5 (library binding)
    1. Tasmanian devil — Juvenile literature. I. Title.
QL737.M33S57 2010
599.2'7 — dc22   2009040494

Editorial Credits
Gillia Olson, editor; Bobbie Nuytten, designer; Wanda Winch, media researcher; Eric Manske, production specialist

Photo Credits
Alamy/Arco Images GmbH/TUNS, 5; Dave Watts, 15; deadlyphoto.com, cover; Gerry Pearce, 11; Mark Eveleigh, 9;
    Rob Walls, 17
Ardea/Auscape/D. Parer & E. Parer-Cook, 7, 19
Getty Images Inc./Adam Pretty, 21
Lochman Transparencies/©Hans and Judy Beste, HJ-221, 13
Shutterstock/Ewan Chesser, 1

Note to Parents and Teachers

The Australian Animals set supports national science standards related to life science. This book
describes and illustrates Tasmanian devils. The images support early readers in understanding
the text. The repetition of words and phrases helps early readers learn new words. This book
also introduces early readers to subject-specific vocabulary words, which are defined in the
Glossary section. Early readers may need assistance to read some words and to use the Table
of Contents, Glossary, Read More, Internet Sites, and Index sections of the book.

Table of Contents

Living in Australia

Australia's island of Tasmania is home to a spooky marsupial. The Tasmanian devil was named for its devilish screeches and growls.

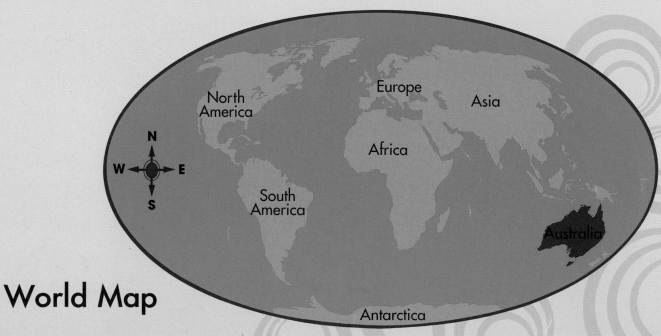

World Map

Tasmanian devils live
in all areas of Tasmania.
They usually hide
in dens during the day.
They come out at night.

Australia
Map

where Tasmanian devils live

Up Close!

Tasmanian devils are about

the size of a small dog.

Their bodies are about

2.5 feet (.8 meter) long.

They have furry tails.

9

Tasmanian devils have black fur.

They often have white markings

on their chests and rumps.

Red ears add

to their devilish look.

Devils have big heads.

Their strong jaws and teeth

crush bones.

Long whiskers help them

find their way in the dark.

A Devil's Life

Young devils live in their

mother's pouch for 15 weeks.

Then they live in the family den.

After eight months,

young devils live on their own.

Finding Food

Tasmanian devils aren't picky.

They will eat any

dead animals they find.

Devils also hunt wallabies,

insects, and lizards.

Staying Safe

Adult devils have few predators.

Young devils usually hide

to stay safe.

They also may climb trees

or use their strong jaws to bite.

A kind of cancer has killed

many Tasmanian devils.

Scientists are working

to help them.

Laws also protect devils.

Glossary

cancer — a disease in which unhealthy cells in the body grow quickly and damage healthy body parts

den — a place where a wild animal lives; a den may be a cave or a hole in the ground or a tree trunk.

jaw — a part of the mouth used to grab, bite, and chew

marsupial — a mammal that carries its young in a pouch

pouch — a pocket of skin; baby Tasmanian devils live in their mother's pouch.

predator — an animal that hunts other animals for food

whisker — a long, stiff hair near the mouth of some mammals

Read More

Hengel, Katherine. *It's a Baby Tasmanian Devil!* Baby Australian Animals. Edina, Minn.: Abdo, 2010.

Markle, Sandra. *Tasmanian Devils.* Animal Scavengers. Minneapolis: Lerner, 2005.

Markovics, Joyce L. *Tasmanian Devil: Nighttime Scavenger.* Uncommon Animals. New York: Bearport, 2009.

Internet Sites

FactHound offers a safe, fun way to find Internet sites related to this book. All of the sites on FactHound have been researched by our staff.

Here's all you do:

Visit *www.facthound.com*

FactHound will fetch the best sites for you!

Index

Word Count: 196
Grade: 1
Early-Intervention Level: 20